SCHIRMER'S LIBRARY OF MUSICAL CLASSICS

Compositions for the Piano
FRÉDÉRIC CHOPIN

Edited, Revised, and Fingered by
RAFAEL JOSEFFY

Historical and Analytical Comments by
JAMES HUNEKER

G. SCHIRMER, Inc.

DISTRIBUTED BY

7777 W. BLUEMOUND RD. P.O. BOX 13819 MILWAUKEE, WI 53213

THE NOCTURNES

HERE is the chronology of the Nocturnes: opus 9, three Nocturnes, January, 1833; opus 15, three Nocturnes, January, 1834; opus 27, two Nocturnes, May, 1836; opus 32, two Nocturnes, December, 1837; opus 37, two Nocturnes, May, 1840; opus 48, two Nocturnes, August, 1841; opus 55, two Nocturnes, August, 1844; opus 62, two Nocturnes, September, 1846. In addition there is a Nocturne written in 1828 and published by Fontana, with the opus number 72, No. 2, and one in C sharp minor, discovered later, written when Chopin was young, and published in 1895.

John Field has been described as the forerunner of Chopin. The limpid style of this pupil and friend of Clementi, and his beautiful touch and finished execution, were admired by the Pole. The nocturnes of Field are now neglected, though without warrant; not only is he the creator of the form, but in his nocturnes and concertos he has written sweet and sane music. Field rather patronized Chopin, with whose melancholy pose he had no patience. "He has a sick-room talent," growled the Irishman in the intervals between his wine-drinking, pipe-smoking, and the washing of his linen—the latter economical habit he had contracted from Clementi. There is some truth in this stricture. Chopin, seldom exuberantly cheerful, is in many of his Nocturnes morbidly sad and complaining. The most admired of his compositions, with the exception of his Waltzes, they are in several instances his weakest. Nevertheless, he ennobled the form originated by Field, giving it dramatic breadth, passion, even grandeur. Set against Field's naïve and idyllic specimens the efforts of Chopin are too often bejewelled, far too lugubrious, too tropical—Asiatic is a better word; and they have the exotic savor of the heated conservatory, not the fresh scent of the flowers grown in the open by the less poetic John Field. And then Chopin is so desperately sentimental at times. Some of these compositions are not altogether to the taste of the present generation; they seem anæmic in feeling. However, there are a few noble Nocturnes, and some methods of performance may have much to answer for in the sentimentalizing of the others. More vigor, a quickening of the time-pulse, and a less languishing touch, will rescue them from lush sentimentality. Chopin loved the night and its starry mysteries; his Nocturnes are true night-pieces, some wearing an agitated, remorseful countenance; others seen in profile only; while many are like whisperings at dusk—Verlaine moods. The poetic side of men of genius is feminine,

and in Chopin the feminine note was over-emphasized, at moments it was almost hysterical, particularly in these Nocturnes. The Scotch have a proverb: "She wove her shroud and wore it in her lifetime." The shroud is not far away in the Nocturnes. Chopin wove his till the day of his death; and he sometimes wore it—but not always, as many persons believe.

Among the elegaic of his Nocturnes is the first in B flat minor; of far more significance than its two companions, it is, for some reason, neglected. While I am far from agreeing with those who hold that in the early Chopin his genius was completely revealed, yet this Nocturne is as striking as the last Nocturne; it is at once sensuous and dramatic, melancholy and lovely. Emphatically a gray mood. The section in octaves is exceedingly seductive. As a melody it contains all the mystic crooning and lurking voluptuousness of its composer. There is throughout flux and reflux, passion peeping out in the *coda*. The E flat Nocturne is graceful, shallow in content, but if it is played with purity of tone and freedom from sentimentalism it is not nearly as banal as it seems. It is Field-like, therefore play it, as did Rubinstein, in Field-like fashion. Hadow calls attention to the "remote and recondite modulations" in the twelfth bar, the chromatic double-notes. For him they are the only real modulation; "the rest of the passage is an iridescent play of color, an effect of superficies, not an effect of substance." It was the E flat Nocturne that unloosed Rellstab's critical wrath in the "Iris." Of it he wrote: "Where Field smiles, Chopin makes a grinning grimace; where Field sighs, Chopin groans," and so on, a string of antitheses, witty but irrelevant, ending with the rather comical plea: "We implore Mr. Chopin to return to nature." Rellstab might have added that, while Field is often commonplace, Chopin never is. Gracious, even coquettish, is the first part of the B major Nocturne of this opus. Well knit, the passionate intermezzo has the true dramatic ring. It should be taken *alla breve*. The ending is quite effective.

I do not care very much for the F major Nocturne. This opus 15 is dedicated to Ferdinand Hiller. Ehlert speaks of "the ornament in triplets with which he brushes the theme as with the gentle wings of a butterfly," and then discusses the artistic value of the ornament which may be so profitably studied in the Chopin music. "From its nature, the ornament can only beautify the beautiful." Music like Chopin's, with its predominating elegance, could not forgo ornament.

25438

Ehlert thinks that the F sharp major Nocturne is inseparable from champagne and truffles. It is more elegant, also more dramatic than the one in F major, which precedes it. That, with the exception of the middle part in F minor, is weak, though pretty and confiding. The F sharp major Nocturne is popular. The *doppio movimento* is extremely striking, the entire piece saturated with young life, love and feeling of good-will to mankind. The third Nocturne of this opus is in G minor and exhibits picturesque writing. There is not much of the fantastic, yet the languid earth-weary voice of the opening and the churchly refrain of the chorale—is there not here fantastic contrast! This Nocturne contains in solution all that Chopin developed in a later Nocturne of the same key. I think the first stronger, its lines simpler, more primitive, its coloring less varied, yet quite as rich and gloomy. Of it Chopin on being interrogated for its key said: "After Hamlet," but changing his mind added, "Let them guess for themselves." A sensible conclusion. Kullak's programme is conventional. It is the lament for the beloved one, the lost Lenore, with religious consolation thrown in as a make-weight. The bell-tones of the plain-chant evoke for me little that is consoling, though the piece ends in the major mode. It is more like Poe's "Ulalume." A tiny tone-poem, Anton Rubinstein made much of it. In the seventeenth bar and during four bars there is a held note, F, and I once heard the Russian virtuoso keep this tone prolonged by some miraculous means. The *tempo* is very slow, and the tone is not in a position where the sustaining pedal can sensibly help it. Yet under Rubinstein's velvet fingers it swelled and diminished, and went on singing into the E as if the instrument were an organ. I suppose the inaudible changing of fingers on the note, with his artistic pedalling, achieved the wonderful effect.

The next Nocturne opus 27, No. 1, brings us to a masterpiece. With the possible exception of the C minor Nocturne, this one in the sombre key of C sharp minor is a great essay in the form. Kleczynski finds it "a description of a calm night at Venice, where, after a scene of murder, the sea closes over a corpse and continues to mirror the moonlight"; which is melodramatic. The wide meshed figure of the left hand supports a morbid, persistent melody that grates on the nerves. From the *più mosso* the agitation increases, and just here note the Beethovenish quality of these bars, which continues till the change of key-signature. There is a surprising climax followed by sunshine in the D flat part; then, after mounting dissonances, a bold succession of octaves leads to the feverish plaint of the opening. The composition attains exalted states; its psychologic tension is at times so great as to lead the hearer to the border of the pathologic. There is fantastic power in this Nocturne, which is seldom interrupted with sinister subtlety. Henry T. Finck rightfully

believes it "embodies a greater variety of emotion and more genuine dramatic spirit on four pages than many operas on four hundred." The companion picture in D flat, opus 27, No. 2, has, as Karasowski writes, "a profusion of delicate *fioriture.*" It contains but one subject and is an intimate song; there is obvious meaning in the duality of voices. Often heard in the concert room, this Nocturne gives us a surfeit of thirds and sixths in elaborate ornamentation, and a certain monotone of mood; and it is an imploring melody, harmonically interesting. A curious marking in the older editions, and usually overlooked by pianists, is the *crescendo* and *con forza* of the little cadenza. This is evidently erroneous. The theme should first be *piano*, and on its return *pianissimo* and *forte*, respectively, according to Kleczynski.

The best part of the next Nocturne—B major, opus 32, No. 1—is the *coda*; it is in minor and is like the drumbeat of tragedy. The entire ending, a stormy recitative, is in stern contrast to the dreamy beginning. The Nocturne that follows, in A flat, is a reversion to the Field type, the opening recalling that master's B flat major nocturne. The F minor section of Chopin's broadens out to dramatic reaches, but as an entirety this opus is not particularly noteworthy. The Nocturne in G minor, opus 37, No. 1, is much admired. The chorale, said Chopin's pupil. Gutmann, is taken too slowly, its composer having forgotten to mark the increased tempo. The Nocturne in G is exquisite. Painted with the most ethereal brush, without the cloying splendors of the D flat Nocturne, the double-thirds, fourths and sixths are magically euphonious. The second subject is one of the most beautiful penned by Chopin. It has the true barcarolle atmosphere, and subtle are the shifting harmonic hues. Pianists usually take the first part too fast, the second too slow, transposing the poetic composition into an agile étude. Both numbers of this opus are without dedications. They are the offspring of the trip to Majorca.

The Nocturne in C minor, opus 48, No. 1, has its despairing moments, but it is the broadest, most imposing and most dramatic of the series; its middle movement is a departure from the form. Biggest in conception, it is a miniature music-drama. Adequately to interpret it demands the grand manner. The *doppio movimento* is dramatically exciting. A fitting pendant is this composition to the C sharp minor Nocturne. Both works display the heroic quality, both are free from mawkishness, and are Chopin in the mode masculine. The following Nocturne No. 2, in F sharp minor, is poetic and contains a fine recitative in D flat. It was a favorite of its composer. Opus 55, two Nocturnes in F minor and E flat major, need no longer detain us. The first is familiar. Kleczynski devotes a page or more to its execution. He asks us to vary the return of the chief subject with nuances, as would an artistic singer the couplets of a classic song. There are "cries of despair" in it, but at last "a feeling of hope." It is the relief of a major key after prolonged wandering in the minor. Not epoch-making, it is a nice Nocturne, and neat in its sorrow. The succeeding example gives "the impression of an improvisation."

Opus 62 brings us to a pair in the respective keys of B and E major. The first, the so-called Tuberose Nocturne, is faint with a sickly, yet rich odor. The climbing trellis of notes that so unexpectedly leads to the tonic, is a fascinating surprise, and the chief tune has a fruity charm. The piece is highly ornate, its harmonies dense, the entire surface overruns with wild ornamentation and a profusion of trills. This Nocturne, the third of its kind in the key of B, is not easy; and though unduly luxuriant it deserves warmer praise than has been accorded it. Irregular as is its outline, its troubled lyrism is appealing, is melting, and the A flat portion with its timid, hesitating accents is very attractive. The following, the E major Nocturne, has the authentic Bardic ring. Its song is almost declamatory, the intermediate portion is both wavering and passionate. The work shows no decrease in creative vigor

or lyric fancy. The posthumous Nocturne in E minor, composed in 1827, is rather pale yet sweet; it contains some very un-Chopinlike modulations. The C sharp minor, published two decades ago, is hardly a treasure-trove. It is vague and reminiscent. The original manuscript is in Chopin's handwriting; the piece was first played at the Chopin Commemoration concert in the autumn of 1894, at Zelazowa-Wola, and afterward at Warsaw by the Russian composer and pianist, Balakirev. This Nocturne was sent to his sister Louise at Warsaw in a letter from Warsaw, and was supposedly destroyed during the sacking of the Zamajski palace at Warsaw in 1863, but was saved and published. It is a romantic story, and true or not, doesn't much matter, because of the musical mediocrity of the composition. Is this the Nocturne of which Tausig spoke to his pupil, Rafael Joseffy, as belonging to the master's best period, or did he refer to the one in E minor?

James Huneker

Thematic Index

Edited and fingered by
Rafael Joseffy

3

à Madame Camilla Pleyel

Nocturne

F. Chopin. Op. 9, № 1

Larghetto (♩ = 116.)

1.

Copyright, 1915, by G. Schirmer, Inc.
Copyright renewed, 1943, by G. Schirmer, Inc.

25438

25438

Edited and fingered by
Rafael Josefty

8

a Madame Camilla Pleyel

Nocturne

F. CHOPIN. Op. 9, № 2

2.

25438

Edited and fingered by
Rafael Joseffy

a Madame Camilla Pleyel

Nocturne

F. Chopin. Op. 9, № 3

3.

25438

à Mr Ferdinand Hiller

Nocturne

Edited and fingered by
Rafael Joseffy

F. Chopin. Op. 15, Nº 1

25438

a M.r Ferdinand Hiller

Nocturne

Edited and fingered by
Rafael Joseffy

Larghetto (♩=40)

F. Chopin. Op. 15, № 2

5.

sostenuto

25438

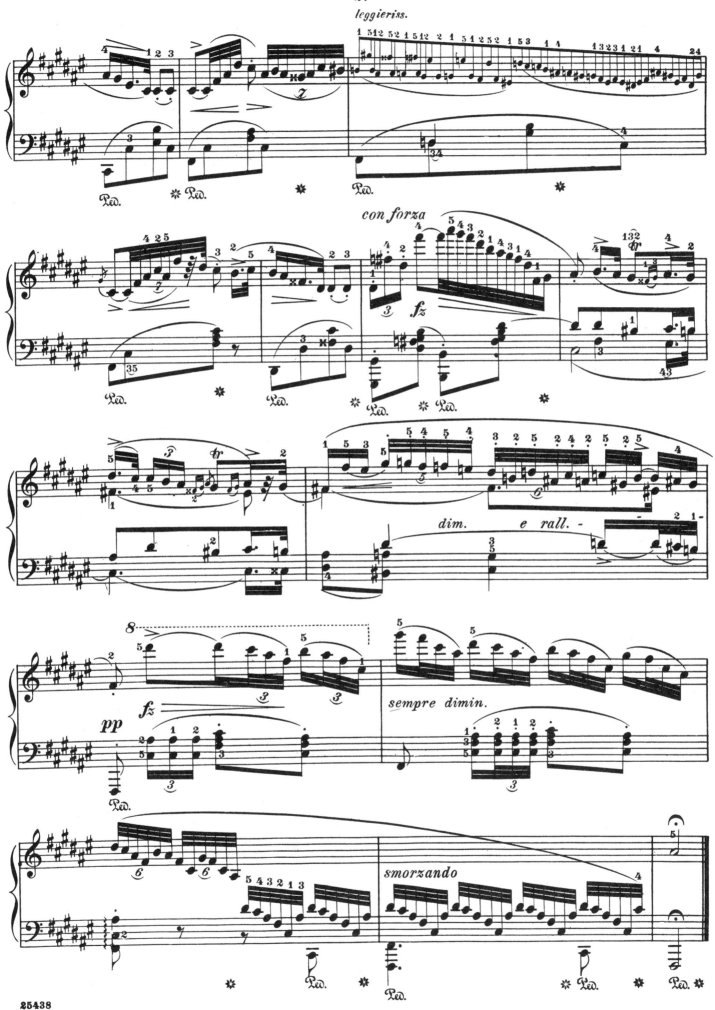

à M.ª Ferainand Hiller

Nocturne

Edited and fingered by
Rafael Joseffy

F. Chopin. Op. 15, № 3

6.

25438

à Mme la Comtesse d'Appony

Nocturne

Edited and fingered by
Rafael Joseffy

F. Chopin. Op. 27, Nº 1

à Mme la Comtesse d'Appony

Nocturne

Edited and fingered by
Rafael Joseffy

F. Chopin. Op. 27, № 2

Lento sostenuto (♩.= 50)

8.

25438

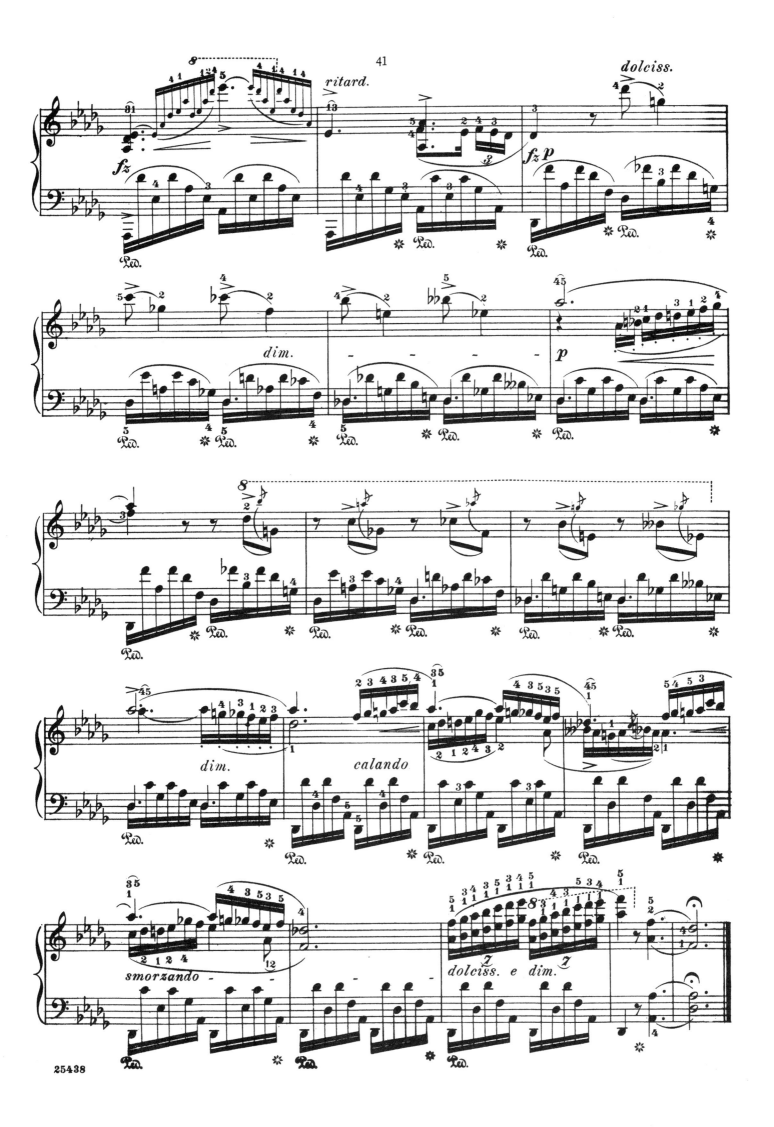

**Edited and fingered by
Rafael Joseffy**

à Mᵐᵉ la Baronne de Billing, née de Courbonne

Nocturne

Andante sostenuto

F. Chopin. Op. 32, Nº 1

Copyright, 1915, by G. Schirmer, Inc.
Copyright renewed, 1943, by G. Schirmer, Inc.

à Mme la Baronne de Billing, née de Courbonne

Nocturne

Edited and fingered by
Rafael Joseffy

F. Chopin. Op. 32, № 2

10.

25438

25438

Edited and fingered by
Rafael Joseffy

Nocturne

F. Chopin. Op. 37, № 1.

Andante sostenuto

11.

25438

Nocturne

Edited and fingered by
Rafael Josoffy

F. Chopin. Op. 37, No. 2

Andantino

12.

dolce

legato

25438

57

25438　　*) **Dieser Takt ist in der Klindworth Ausgabe weggelassen.**

à Mademoiselle Laura Duperré

Nocturne

Edited and fingered by
Rafael Joseffy

F. Chopin. Op. 48, No 1

13.

25438

à Mademoiselle Laura Duperré.

Nocturne

Edited and fingered by
Rafael Joseffy

F. Chopin. Op. 48, № 2

25438

25438

Klindworth:

Edited and fingered by
Rafael Joseffy

à Mlle J. W. Stirling

Nocturne

F. Chopin. Op. 55, N° 1.

Andante

15.

25438

25438

à Mlle J. W Stirling

Nocturne

Edited and fingered by
Rafael Joseffy

Lento sostenuto

F. Chopin. Op. **55**, No. 2

16.

25438

Edited and fingered by
Rafael Joseffy

à Mademoiselle R. de Könneritz

Nocturne

F. Chopin. Op. 62, No. 1

17.

25438

25438

Edited and fingered by
Rafael Joseffy

à Mademoiselle R. de Könneritz

Nocturne

F. Chopin. Op. 62, № 2

Lento
sostenuto

18.

25438

25438

Nocturne

Posthumous

Edited and fingered by
Rafael Joseffy

F. Chopin. Op. 72, № 1
(1827)

19.

25438

25438

25438